PC

GILLIAN RICHARDSON

kaboom!

EXPLOSIONS OF ALL KINDS

W9-ABY-983

annick press
toronto + new york + vancouver

To my RR family, for the inspiration of their awesome creative energy and their generous support

Annick Press Ltd.

Edited by Kim Aippersbach
Copyedited by Laura Edlund
Proofread by Geri Rowlatt
Cover and interior design by Irvin Cheung/iCheung Design, inc.
Cover photograph: Mike Kemp/Rubberball Productions/Getty Images

We acknowledge the support of the Canada Council for the Arts, the Ontario Arts Council, and the Government of Canada through the Book Publishing Industry Development Program (BPIDP) for our publishing activities.

ONTARIO ARTS COUNCIL
CONSEIL DES ARTS DE L'ONTARIO

Cataloguing in Publication
Richardson, Gillian
    Kaboom! : explosions of all kinds / by Gillian Richardson.
Includes bibliographical references and index.

ISBN 978-1-55451-204-1 (bound).—ISBN 978-1-55451-203-4 (pbk.)
    1. Explosions—Juvenile literature. I. Title.

QD516.R53 2009   j541'.361   C2009-901099-2

Printed and bound in China

Published in the U.S.A. by	Distributed in Canada by	Distributed in the U.S.A. by
Annick Press (U.S.) Ltd.	Firefly Books Ltd.	Firefly Books (U.S.) Inc.
	66 Leek Crescent	P.O. Box 1338
	Richmond Hill, ON	Ellicott Station
	L4B 1H1	Buffalo, NY 14205

Visit our website at **www.annickpress.com**

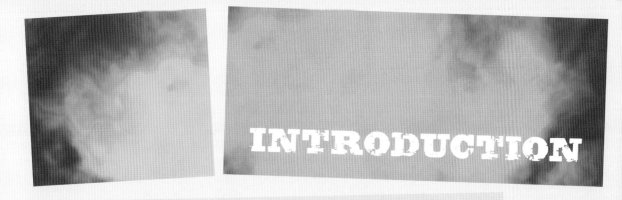

INTRODUCTION

A volcano blows its top in a violent eruption. Sticks of dynamite blast apart after a fuse is lit. A firecracker bursts open with a loud *bang*, showering multicolored sparks from the night sky. We call all of these events "explosions." And their power can be stunning. The *boom* from a fireworks display rattles windows. A tall concrete building will collapse in a huge dust cloud after explosive charges destroy the inside walls. Amazingly, the shock wave from a volcano erupting is strong enough to knock down a forest miles away.

What causes all that power and noise? An explosion happens when there is a rapid release of energy, usually because gases that are under extreme pressure suddenly need more space. They push with great force against whatever is holding them back. When the explosion finally happens, and the container bursts, there's usually a loud *bang*.

Take popcorn, for example. This puffed-up, crunchy food starts out as a hard kernel of corn. How does it become the treat we know? By simply adding heat to popcorn kernels, you start a chain reaction that ends in an explosion. Inside that hard outer coating—called a "hull"—is a moist, starchy substance. When it's heated to 200 degrees C (400 degrees F), the moisture turns to steam. Just as pressure builds up in a pot of boiling water and the lid begins to dance—or if you shake a bottle of soda—pressure builds up in the corn kernel. Once that pressure becomes too much, the kernel blows itself inside out with a *pop!* That's the sound of the outer shell cracking open and the steam rushing out. Your snack is ready!

An explosion happens every time you heat a popcorn kernel until it bursts open.

After rising 18,000 meters (60,000 feet), ash from the eruption of Mount St. Helens volcano in Washington State drifted as far east as the Great Lakes.

Explosions can also happen when highly flammable material catches fire suddenly. This process, called "combustion," produces heat, light, and large amounts of gases, such as carbon dioxide and nitrogen. The speed at which hot gases are created is the power behind an explosion. Slowly burning material, like wood, doesn't explode because the heat and gases aren't moving fast enough to create high pressure. However, the material in gunpowder and dynamite ignites so quickly that the expanding gas can propel a bullet or shatter granite. The same process powers your car, but it is safely contained inside the engine.

Explosions that happen naturally may be destructive, but they can also help to create new things. Volcanoes around the world have destroyed forests and homes. They have also formed new land with cooled, hardened lava. Massive explosions of stars may reveal the secrets of how the universe began.

An explosion sends a fireworks rocket to a pre-set height where it will explode again with color and sound.

Not all explosions have to involve fire and heat, bangs or destruction. "Explosive" words that we use every day let people know something happened suddenly, passionately, or maybe unexpectedly. You might *erupt* with laughter at a hilarious scene in a movie. Does your friend have an *explosive* temper that is easily triggered if he doesn't get what he wants. Did your mom *blow up* when she saw the mess you left after making pizza? Did you eat so much you thought you'd *burst* or *explode*? At the best parties, you might have a *blast*!

EXPLOSIVE WORDS!

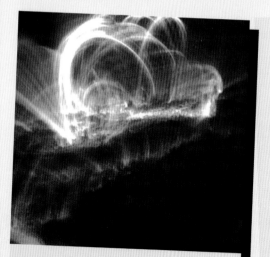

Scientific instruments can measure the amount of radiation released by powerful solar flares from our sun.

People sometimes use explosions to destroy. For example, bombs are weapons intended to cause death and devastation. Yet people also use explosions in positive ways. Dynamite blows up unwanted rock or unsafe buildings, leaving room for new construction. Fireworks dazzle us with an amazing show of light, color, and sound.

Natural or artificial, explosions happen in space and on Earth, in dramatic events and everyday life. Whenever and wherever they occur, they have the power to startle us, excite us, or simply make us curious.

explosions in nature

DOWN TO EARTH 1

Volcanoes

Volcanoes can be the most violent explosions on Earth, erupting without warning and causing sudden, widespread devastation. The volcanic island of Krakatoa used to rise 450 meters (1,475 feet) out of the sea near the Indonesian island of Java. In August 1883, the volcano exploded and collapsed so that much of it sank below sea level. Krakatoa's explosion was so violent that it sent up an ash cloud 80 kilometers (50 miles) in the sky, was heard over 3,200 kilometers (2,000 miles) away in Australia, and is estimated as having had five times the power of a nuclear bomb.

While few people saw the eruption, many suffered. The island of Krakatoa itself was uninhabited, but the eruption caused a tsunami, or tidal wave, that raced across the sea at a height of 40 meters (130 feet), destroying 163 coastal villages and killing 36,000 people.

What caused Krakatoa to erupt so explosively?

Beneath a volcano, gases and a mass of molten rock called "magma" are heated by Earth's superhot core. If the magma stays hot enough, it can escape from the top of the volcano as flows or spurts of lava. This is how the Hawaiian islands were formed, with slow additions of lava over hundreds of thousands of years. But sometimes the magma is thicker, moves slower, and may cool enough to form a plug that blocks the top of the cone— like a cork in a bottle. Behind the plug, magma and hot gases continue to build up an enormous amount of pressure, waiting for an event that will cause the volcano to blow its top.

An artist's illustration shows how Krakatoa might have looked when it began to erupt in 1883.

A scientist measures the gases rising from magma in a lava vent on Kilauea Volcano on Hawaii's Big Island.

For a volcano, the action that sends that pent-up hot stuff through the roof might be an earthquake, which would allow a sudden release of pressure through new cracks in the mountain. Or it could be the arrival of water, which will trigger a rapid expansion of the magma and gas as it creates steam. Water, steam, and *boom*!—water triggering the explosion may be what happened with Krakatoa. The plates of Earth's crust move unpredictably under the South Pacific; scientists aren't sure, but they think plate movements created cracks in the walls of the volcano, allowing seawater to flow into the chamber of magma. The sudden expansion of gas would have blasted the island apart.

Whatever the trigger for a particular volcano, it allows the incredible energy of all the built-up pressure to escape suddenly. If the explosive result rips the top off the volcano, it fires hot cinders, dust, and chunks of rock—known as "volcanic bombs"—high into the air. Clouds of ash billow upward and spread far across the skies. Avalanches of rock race down the sides of the volcano. Even more devastating are the mudflows, which can form when hot magma melts mountain glaciers or during intense rainfall. Volcanic eruptions with mudflows are the most dangerous!

In recent history, violent volcanic explosions have killed many and changed the face of the land around them. There were few observers when Krakatoa blew, but in 1980, in Washington State, Mount St. Helens's violent eruption was predicted accurately enough that scientists had cameras ready to record it.

After sleeping for 123 years, Mount St. Helens rumbled to life with an earthquake in March. Many smaller tremors followed and volcanologists knew something was up. A bulge of rock appeared on the north side of the mountain and worried scientists for weeks. They cleared the area of most people, but left a few scientists to keep watch. They measured the ground temperature and kept close tabs on how fast the bulge grew and what kind of gases were escaping from it.

Mount St. Helens had an almost perfect cone-shaped peak before it erupted in 1980.

Visitors to the Mount St. Helens National Volcanic Monument can see the crater left by the explosive eruption.

Even though volcanologists expected an eruption, the way it happened took them by surprise. On May 18, an earthquake rattled the earth 1.6 kilometers (1 mile) below the mountain, and the north side began to collapse into a crater. Without further warning, the mountain blasted sideways, sending rock and ash flying and a shock wave of energy tearing across the land. It flattened 595 square kilometers (230 square miles) of forest. The opening in the crater allowed pulverized, partially molten rock to pour out over ice and snow, melting it rapidly and sending mudflows hurtling down the Toutle River valley. In all, 57 people died.

If it hadn't been for the scientists' close observations and predictions, the death toll would have been much greater. We cannot stop a volcano from erupting, but the more we learn about them, the more we can protect ourselves from their most devastating effects.

KRAKATOA RISES AGAIN!

In 1927, people who were fishing spotted bubbles of steam and rubble in the ocean, showing that the submerged volcano was still active. A year later the rim of a cone-shaped mountain appeared, and soon grew to a small island called Anak Krakatau—or "child of Krakatoa." This "child" continues to erupt—not with the same violence as in 1883, but with lava and rocky material that is creating new land.

Geysers!

Not all explosive eruptions from the earth spew lava or hot molten rock. Not all of them are destructive or deadly. Some are actually entertaining, attracting crowds of people who line up for the show. You've likely heard of Old Faithful, in Wyoming, in Yellowstone National Park. This geyser regularly sends up hot water and steam in sudden spouts 30–60 meters (100–200 feet) high. That could be about as high as a 20-story building.

Geysers can't just pop up anywhere. They need exactly the right ingredients: a constant source of underground heat, a water supply, and a place for that water to collect so it can be heated. A river flowing into an underground pool and hot, solid rocks or magma of an ancient volcanic site to heat the water are perfect. Most of Earth's geysers are in Yellowstone, an area that was formed by many volcanoes long ago. Russia, Chile, New Zealand, and Iceland also have geysers.

A geyser's eruption is actually an explosion of steam created when a large amount of stored water reaches boiling temperature and turns to steam. Because steam needs 1600 times more space than water, you can imagine what must happen. To escape from its underground chamber, the steam forces its way through the closest vent it can find and up to the surface. It appears suddenly as a column or fountain of frothy water and superheated steam—superheated because the boiling point of water is higher the deeper the water is below Earth's surface. Water may reach 230 degrees C (450 degrees F) before it becomes steam. When it suddenly finds a way to the surface...look out!

Strokkur is one of Iceland's geysers. Hot water from underground is used to heat 70 percent of the country's buildings.

Due to a long-term drought, which has reduced the underground water supply, intervals between Old Faithful's eruptions are growing longer.

FUN FACT

Steamboat Geyser in Yellowstone holds the record for the tallest eruptions—91 meters (300 feet)—but you'd be lucky to see one. Steamboat has only performed 10 times in the last 20 years. The news is even worse for Waimangu Geyser in New Zealand. A landslide in 1902 put a stop to its spectacular 488-meter (1,600-foot) steam explosions.

An earthquake could change underground water movement and increase the frequency of Steamboat Geyser's eruptions.

Geysers shoot out spectacular towers of steam over and over again. Old Faithful's spurts can be predicted within about 20 minutes. How? As the geyser runs out of steam, it's like a kettle of water needing to be refilled. Refilling can take time, but in the case of Old Faithful, it only takes about 90 minutes. Once again, the water is heated until it becomes steam and escapes. The steam spout goes on until the boiling kettle is mostly empty, and the cycle begins all over again. Old Faithful has been shooting out water for as long as anyone knows—between 14,000 and 32,000 liters (3,700–8,400 gallons)—and its eruptions were first recorded in 1870.

Coal Mine Methane

Digging for coal in an underground mine has always been dangerous work. One of the biggest hazards for miners is methane, a flammable gas that occurs naturally in small pockets within the coal bed. It only takes small concentrations of it to explode when mixed with oxygen. Miners call the menace "firedamp."

Around 1903, these coal miners on a dinner break kept the Davy lamp burning to warn of methane gas.

In the early days of mining history, explosions regularly occurred deep underground as rock was broken up and methane was set free. Even if the blast itself didn't kill the miners, they had little time to escape the toxic carbon monoxide gas created in mine explosions. In the 1800s, two explosions in England's Tyneside coal mines killed over 250 miners. To try to prevent such accidents, the mine "fireman" would be dressed in dampened clothing and sent to walk through the tunnels with a lit candle at the end of a long stick. Holding the candle up close to the roof would set fire to any traces of methane that collected there, effectively removing it before it built up to dangerous levels. But imagine the risk if the fireman came upon a large pocket of the gas!

What makes methane one of the deadliest risks lurking in those tunnels far below the surface is that miners can't see, smell, taste, or feel it. As miners break up the coal and dig it out of the ground, methane is invisibly released. It drifts up to the roof of the tunnels because it is lighter than air. Even small proportions of methane to air (5–15 percent methane) can be ignited by a flame or even a spark caused by electricity or the friction of a metal tool hitting rock. Because methane catches fire quickly, an explosion results.

A methane explosion can also set off a coal-dust explosion because coal dust is easily ignited. Work in a mine stirs up coal dust, so mine safety workers have to use fans to bring in fresh air to reduce the concentration of methane and coal dust, and flush the dust out from the work areas. The worst mine disaster

Mines are a lot safer now than they used to be, but methane explosions are still a risk.

in history happened in 1942, in China, when 1,572 miners died in a massive coal-dust explosion.

In today's coal mines, sensitive instruments can detect methane in tunnels. If even 1 percent is found, electrical and mechanical equipment is shut down until the deadly gas can be removed. Even with sophisticated safety measures, accidents still occur in mines. In January 2006, a fatal methane explosion in the Sago Mine in West Virginia trapped 11 miners behind barricades.

Sir Humphrey Davy invented a safety lamp for miners in 1817. The lamp provided light, but also helped the mine fireman search for methane. The Davy lamp was fueled by oil and enclosed the flame with a screen of fine wire mesh. As small amounts of methane entered through the mesh, the lamp flame would burn the gas off safely inside the lamp.

THE HINDENBURG

A witness to the *Hindenburg* tragedy photographed the explosion, caused by flames igniting the airship's hydrogen gas cells.

Imagine the thrill of sailing in near-silence through the clouds, held aloft by a big bag of lighter-than-air gas. Dirigibles, or airships, were once the hottest thing in passenger travel. But what happened to the most famous of these airships brought an abrupt end to this exciting style of travel.

The LZ 129 *Hindenburg* was the largest of these amazing aircraft, completed in 1936 at a cost of $2.5 million (US) and named for the late German president Paul von Hindenburg. At 245 meters (804 feet) long, it was almost as long as four and a half of today's space shuttles parked nose to tail. Inside the treated cotton skin that stretched over an aluminum frame, 16 giant bags held the hydrogen gas used for lift. Powered by four engines, the *Hindenburg*'s top speed of 135 kilometers

(84 miles) per hour could take it across the Atlantic in two and a half days, almost twice as fast as the speediest ocean liner at that time. In fact, the *Hindenburg* once set a record in 1936 for a return crossing in just 5 days, 19 hours, and 51 minutes. The airship was a star feature at the opening ceremonies of the Berlin Olympics in 1936.

ZEPPELINS!

After 17 trans-Atlantic return trips in its first season, the *Hindenburg* left Frankfurt, Germany, on May 3, 1937. The airship had a crew of 61, and 36 passengers had booked the individual small cabins. Only the wealthy could afford the $400 (US) tickets, a great deal of money at the time. Passengers ate elaborate meals in a central dining room and spent most of their time relaxing in a comfortable lounge during the flight. The ship was due to land in the afternoon of May 6 at Lakehurst Naval Air Station in Manchester, New Jersey. A late arrival and bad weather closing in made the landing trickier than usual. The ship

moved into position to lower a mooring line by winch from the nose to a tower.

Suddenly, flames erupted near the top fin of the airship. The fire appeared to explode on the balloon's shell and spread forward quickly, causing the frame to break and the ship to drop, rear end first. Collapsing on the ground only 34 seconds after the first flame was seen, the enormous airship was crushed and consumed by fire. Of the 36 people who lost their lives, 13 were passengers and 22 were crew members, many of whom had tried to help passengers to safety. One member of the ground crew was also killed. Most people who died had jumped from the burning aircraft. Others who stayed on board until it crashed were able to run to safety.

The spectacular, fiery end of the *Hindenburg* also meant the end of dirigibles as passenger airliners. Naturally, people were afraid to fly in them. The cause of the fire has never been completely solved. Some experts believe either the hydrogen gas being released to help lower the airship or the combustible coating on the outside of the balloon caught fire somehow. Hydrogen is flammable when mixed with oxygen, and the *Hindenburg* was originally designed to use non-flammable helium to give it lift. But the United States, which was the only country producing helium at the time, refused to sell it to Germany during events that built up to World War II.

Although the tragedy of the *Hindenburg* made explosive, unforgettable headlines, you'll still see dirigibles flying today. Look up at a major outdoor sports event and the television cameras will likely be peering down from a blimp. Small versions of these airships are also used as flying billboards for advertising. The most exciting news, though, may be the recent revival of passenger airship cruises in Europe by the original German company, Zeppelin. Imagine taking a flight through the clouds, held high by a big bag of lighter-than-air–and now safely non-flammable helium–gas!

While powered airships date back to the 1850s, Count Ferdinand von Zeppelin invented an aluminum-framed dirigible in Germany in the late 19th century. Zeppelins were used briefly in World War I for reconnaissance and as bombers, but they became better known following the war for a peaceful purpose. With their efficient cigar shape to aid steering, gasoline engines for power, and a gondola beneath to carry passengers, these rigid balloons became the first passenger aircraft to fly across the Atlantic Ocean from Europe to North America and South America in the 1920s and 1930s.

OUTER SPACE

The Big Bang

Once upon a time, there was no universe. Hold on! That's pretty hard to imagine.

If it didn't exist, how did it begin? When did it happen? What's happening now? Will it end? These are questions that have always puzzled astronomers (who study outer space) and physicists (who study energy, what things are made of, and how they behave). For centuries, people believed that stars were pinholes of light in a dark shell that surrounded Earth. What would those people think today about the Big Bang Theory—the idea that the universe began with a gigantic explosion of matter that is still hurtling through space from the force of the blast that started it all?

How did this amazing idea come into being? Georges Lemaître, a Belgian astrophysicist, studied the work of astronomer Edwin Hubble and Albert Einstein's theory of how space, time, and matter are connected. Lemaître first suggested in 1927 that the universe came into being all at once when a mass of matter broke apart in a superheated explosion. His idea led to even more questions. How could anyone prove this? Hubble (yes, the Hubble Space Telescope is named for him) was the first to find evidence that objects in space are moving away from each other. Using a telescope, he measured the distances to smaller and larger galaxies outside our galaxy, the Milky Way, to show how they were expanding in all directions.

The idea of the universe expanding from its beginnings between 12 and 14 billion years ago was given the name "Big Bang Theory" in the 1950s by Russian-born physicist George

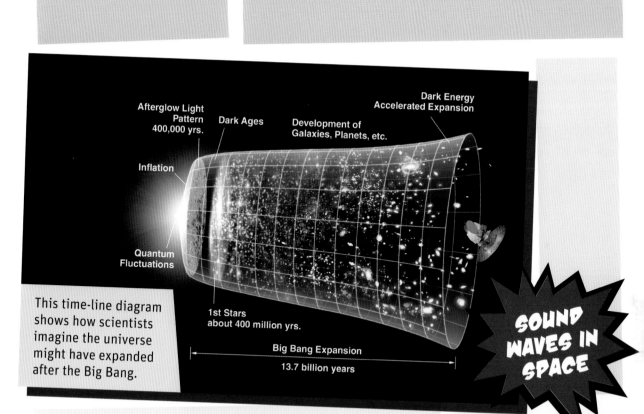

Afterglow Light
Pattern
400,000 yrs.

Dark Ages

Development of
Galaxies, Planets, etc.

Dark Energy
Accelerated Expansion

Inflation

Quantum
Fluctuations

1st Stars
about 400 million yrs.

Big Bang Expansion

13.7 billion years

This time-line diagram shows how scientists imagine the universe might have expanded after the Big Bang.

SOUND WAVES IN SPACE

If massive explosions happen in space, why don't we hear them? Sound waves need a substance to travel through. Water and Earth's atmosphere are good conductors of sound, but the environment in space is so thin that not enough particles of matter are present to carry sounds well. Scientists have heard space noise picked up by super-sensitive microphones, but our ears alone can't detect them.

Gamow. His work showed that, as space expanded, particles of hot matter began to cool and join together to form hydrogen and helium, both of which are needed for life to exist.

Scientists today point out that calling the Big Bang an "explosion" might give the wrong idea. Perhaps the universe didn't burst apart into pieces from one central spot like a bomb, but rather a tightly formed mass of matter became so hot it suddenly began to spread out in all directions at once. Here's one way to think of this: draw a dot on a balloon before blowing it up; when you blow up the balloon, the dot will get bigger. The dot doesn't move on the surface of the balloon, or break apart, but it swells in all directions. Like other explosions, though, the initial expansion of the universe is thought to have taken mere fractions of a second. With all that speed and power behind so much matter spreading across space, who knows how far and how long it might go on. Forever? By studying the way the universe looks now, scientists hope to learn enough to understand about its past and maybe its future.

Supernovas

The Big Bang may have created the universe in the first place, but other explosions, called "novas," are going on in outer space all the time. The biggest explosions we've ever observed happen when an enormous star dies. These explosions are called "supernovas." They launch material—stardust—into space with incredible force that has been compared to several octillion nuclear bombs! Supernovas cause a burst of radiation that may shine far brighter than the entire Milky Way galaxy for several weeks or months. The light gradually fades, but the stardust will travel far and wide. Astronomers believe some of it created Earth and all the life upon it.

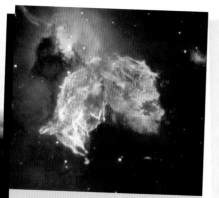

A Hubble Space Telescope image shows the remnant of a supernova in the Large Magellanic Cloud.

How does a star become a supernova? Stars continue to grow as their gravity attracts material from space. Trapped at the core of the star, the material heats up under pressure. A cooking process called "nuclear fusion" is taking place. Once the mass of material reaches a size that is at least eight times larger than our sun, and the hydrogen needed for fusion is all used up, the end is near. The star burns up the other heavy elements until all that is left is iron, which doesn't burn. A tug of war takes place—with gravity pulling in and energy from fusion pushing out. At first, gravity wins and the star collapses inward. But the extra heat and closely packed material soon need to escape: the star explodes violently, scattering bits into space. The death of the biggest stars—more than 15 times the size of our sun—leaves behind what's known as a "black hole."

The material that is ejected from a supernova is composed of the chemical elements needed to create life. Oxygen, carbon, and calcium, as well as heavy elements such as gold, silver, lead, and uranium, combine with the hydrogen and helium already common in the universe. Scientists think that together these form the building blocks for more stars or planets. If so, supernovas could be the keys to all life.

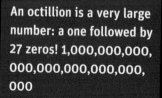

Gas and dust will be all that's left after the death of a star in space.

OCTILLION

An octillion is a very large number: a one followed by 27 zeros! 1,000,000,000, 000,000,000,000,000, 000

Supernovas are rare, especially in our galaxy. We have evidence that they happened in the Milky Way in 1572 and 1604, and astronomers believe the last supernova in our galaxy was over 300 years ago, in 1680. However, scientists can watch these explosions in other galaxies using the Hubble Space Telescope. One supernova called SN1987A, because its light reached Earth in 1987, exploded 169,000 light-years ago in a nearby smaller galaxy called the Large Magellanic Cloud. At the instant of explosion, its light could have been brighter than our whole galaxy. It was visible to the naked eye during 1987 in the southern hemisphere, and while it has faded over time, astronomers can still watch it for changes. Another supernova, SN1993J, was so bright at first that it could be seen without a telescope, but now it can be seen with a telescope in the northern hemisphere. In all, since records were started, about 1,300 supernovas have been sighted.

Why watch a supernova? Tracking its progress over the years can help scientists estimate the amount of matter in the universe, understand how the universe changes, and predict whether it

THE GAMMA RAY BURST!

will keep expanding. The more we know about how our universe works today, the better we can understand its beginnings and possible end.

But don't worry about our sun disappearing as a supernova anytime soon. It should remain mostly unchanged for another 5 billion years before becoming a "white dwarf," the name given to much smaller forms of supernovas.

Light from a gamma ray burst may be 10 to 100 billion times as bright as an entire galaxy.

If you think supernovas are big, meet the gamma ray burst, an explosive flash of high-energy radiation that shoots from the black hole of a dying star 20 or more times bigger than our sun. Astronomers have learned that gamma ray bursts usually come from stars with few heavy metals. The Milky Way galaxy contains loads of metals, so gamma ray bursts are considered a long shot here.

Astronomers first saw the extremely bright light that gamma ray bursts give off in the 1960s. The United States was watching through powerful telescopes to make sure the Soviet Union was obeying the Nuclear Test Ban Treaty. What scientists first thought might be nuclear bombs exploding in outer space were actually super-bright flashes of gamma ray bursts coming from beyond our galaxy, billions of light-years away. In 2005, NASA's Swift satellite detected GRB 050904, the most distant one ever seen. Its light took 13 billion years to reach Earth.

Solar Flares

While mighty explosions occur in neighboring galaxies, that big ball of hydrogen gas we call our sun might appear to hang there, peacefully shining down on Earth. But scientists know differently. The sun is a superhot, constantly churning mass of energy with an explosive temper that sometimes bubbles over. What's happening out there?

Our sun goes through cycles when changes in the magnetic field on its surface create areas, called "sunspots," that are cooler (but still over 6,000 degrees C—or 11,000 degrees F). Energy is suddenly released from sunspots at a rate that may equal one million 100 megaton nuclear explosions. The energy surges outward in a loop, then pulls back, like the repeated reactions of a bungee cord. When the loop breaks, particles of matter—protons and electrons—are hurled into space with a force that can be 10 million times stronger than a volcanic eruption. These huge explosions—the largest in our solar system—are called "solar flares." They create different kinds of radiation, such as radio waves, X-rays, and gamma rays, which can reach Earth's outer atmosphere in as little as eight minutes. That's fast!

Scientists think of solar flares as space weather. When solar flares are at their peak, their energy can bump satellites off their orbits, messing with telecommunications on Earth (phone, radio, and TV) and disrupting the GPS systems that help us find our way around. The energy surges create high currents in the atmosphere that can boost currents in power lines and overload them. They might also cause changes in our climate. When sunspot activity is low, Earth's temperatures appear to be cooler.

Scientists study how loops of energy move on the sun. They may soon be able to predict the length of disruptive magnetic storms caused by solar flares.

Regular observations of sunspots, the source of solar flares, began in 1849. Today, space missions study them.

The polar lights (shown here, photographed in Norway) are called aurora borealis in the northern hemisphere and aurora australis in the southern hemisphere.

One appealing result of solar flares is an increase in the aurora borealis—the northern lights that dance across the skies in vividly colored ribbons. Extra particles reaching Earth from our sun transfer their energy to molecules of nitrogen and oxygen in the atmosphere near Earth's poles. That activity creates the colored light displays we enjoy.

INTENSE SOLAR FLARES!

In 1989, intense solar flares created a high electrical current that damaged major power transformers in Quebec and left millions of people in northeastern North America without electricity for nine hours. Beginning around 2 a.m., power was cut to homes, businesses, city subways, and airports. Newspaper presses ground to a halt. Schools were closed. People driving to work had to cope without traffic lights. Night-shift workers were stuck in elevators. Because Quebec sells power to some US states, they felt the effects of the outages as well.

The International Space Station takes pictures of solar flares.

FUN FACT

Solar flares might be trouble for astronauts on space shuttle flights or at the International Space Station. When solar flare radiation hits the wall of atmosphere surrounding Earth, it isn't able to reach humans directly. However, now that astronauts are spending longer periods of time in outer space, they are at greater risk for the harmful effects of high radiation levels. Scientists will have to find ways to make sure that astronauts aren't taking their space walks when flare activity is high.

DID EXPLOSIONS KILL THE DINOSAURS?

The existence of many complete dinosaur fossils is evidence for paleontologists of a mass extinction.

This mystery may never be solved! The largest known creatures ever to inhabit Earth vanished, along with 60 percent of other living species at about the same time, 65 million years ago. How can we solve a mystery that old?

Look for the first clues in a dinosaur museum: most of the bones come from the K-T boundary—rock layers that mark the end of the Cretaceous age and beginning of the Tertiary age in Earth's history. Few dinosaur fossils younger than this have ever been found. Though it is hard to prove, many scientists believe one or more explosive events could have caused massive extinctions of dinosaurs. In 1980, scientists Luis and Walter Alvarez first proposed the idea that an enormous, superheated asteroid slammed into Earth and set off

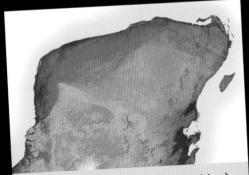

The discovery of a crater (in blue) in Mexico's Yucatán Peninsula convinced many scientists that an asteroid impact led to dinosaur extinction.

the scorching chunks of asteroids, thick smoke would billow into the atmosphere and cause long periods of darkness. Acid rain would poison the water and soil. Heat trapped under the dense clouds may have caused long-term global warming. With less life-giving sunlight, fewer plants would grow. Over time, the remaining enormous dinosaurs would find it harder and harder to find food. The weakened populations would decline, with fewer chances to reproduce. Unable to adapt over time, the dinosaurs would gradually die out.

And, indeed, die out is what they did, but the reasons will never be completely clear. In fact, there is disagreement among scientists about possible reasons. Some think it's more likely that explosive volcanic eruptions caused the extinction, or perhaps dinosaurs faced both volcanic eruptions and an exploding asteroid. It is possible to figure out the date of ancient volcanic lava, so we know that 500,000 years before the dinosaurs disappeared, many volcanoes were active, especially in India. We know that eruptions can throw huge volumes of ash high into the atmosphere. Long-term accumulation of ash could have changed the global climate in a way similar to what an asteroid would. Another clue–iridium–is found in asteroids but is also found in magma from Earth's core, leading some scientists to wonder if volcanoes wiped out the dinosaurs. This is one ancient mystery that will continue to keep scientists investigating–and guessing.

catastrophic climate changes that led to the disappearances of many species.

More evidence! In Mexico's Yucatán Peninsula, geologists studying satellite images spotted curious depressions in the ground, signs of what might be a buried crater. Further detective work revealed a bowl-shaped hole 180 kilometers (112 miles) wide and 900 meters (3,000 feet) deep. The hole's size and high levels of a metal called iridium (levels 30 times higher than usual for Earth) support the idea that a huge asteroid created the crater.

What would the dinosaurs have seen? The explosive impact of a blazing asteroid (or a series of them over many years) 65 million years ago would have killed many creatures outright. Those that remained would have seen skies filled with choking clouds of dust. When fires erupted from

kaboom!

An artist's painting shows how bright the Tunguska asteroid explosion might have looked.

Asteroids are chunks of rocky material, containing iridium, that sometimes enter Earth's atmosphere from outer space. Small pieces rarely make it to the surface of our planet because usually they burn up on the way down. Once in a while, though, a bigger lump will get past our atmospheric barrier and explode in the air or upon impact with Earth. These exploding asteroids are called "bolides" and they can happen several times a year.

Scientists think a mid-air asteroid explosion happened in the remote forests of Siberia, Russia, near the Tunguska River in June 1908. It must have been huge because people living 100 kilometers (62 miles) away reported seeing a fireball, feeling its heat, and hearing a loud *whump* before the shock waves knocked them down. No crater was found, and pieces of the bolide itself were likely consumed in the intense explosion. But trees in an area 50 kilometers (31 miles) in diameter were stripped of branches and scorched, and a much larger area was completely flattened.

PLANT AND ANIMAL EXPLOSIONS

Seed Pods

Beware the squirting cucumber! Nowhere near the scale of exploding asteroids, this ornamental plant's eruption still demands attention. Its seeds grow in a bath of juice inside the plant until the whole thing bursts open, splattering slime and seeds every which way.

The squirting cucumber wouldn't be a good addition to your salad: it's poisonous!

In nature, most seeds aren't carefully planted the way you would plant them in a garden. Instead, they have to take their chances with natural methods—for example, scattered by wind, washed to the ground by rain, eaten by birds, or carried off on the fur of a passing animal. Some plants don't rely on these methods of spreading seeds. Instead, like the squirting cucumber, they get off to an explosive start in life.

The dwarf mistletoe is one plant that goes ballistic. It has whitish berries, containing many small seeds surrounded by slimy liquid. When the seeds are ripe, the swollen berries burst, flinging seeds up to a distance of 15 meters (49 feet) at speeds of up to 100 kilometers (62 miles) per hour. A top major-league pitcher might come close to that speed.

Other plants use exploding pods to distribute their seeds. Plants that belong to the pea family grow their seeds in finger-like pods with a seam along each side. When the pods dry, they split along the seams, twisting or curling at the same time, and tossing the seeds away. The drying of the pod is the explosive trigger this time.

After its seed pods burst open, this plant relies on the wind to carry its seeds away.

This dwarf mistletoe seed shoots away from the plant at high speed.

Pulled tighter and tighter, the plant fibers suddenly let go to release the extra tension. The common broom bush that grows abundantly in Europe and the tall lupine that you might see as a garden flower are two plants with pea-like exploding pods.

Another plant, the quinine bush in Australia, goes an extra step (or three) to make sure its seeds will be planted far and wide. The plant's fruit is a seed pod that emu love to eat—so much so that scientists have found up to 142 seed

FUN FACT

The seeds of the jack pine, a tree found in eastern North America, are only released after a forest fire. The fire's extreme heat expands air inside the cones and forces them open. The jack pine is one of the first trees to take root in the burnt ground.

pods in a single emu dropping. Because the emu is a flightless bird, it wanders away and leaves its droppings everywhere. Then, in the hot Australian sun, the droppings dry and the pods burst apart. That's not the end of the story! Next in line for those seeds are ants, which carry them off to their nests, where some are bound to sprout. More bushes! Now that's a well-managed planting program!

Perhaps the best-named plant that uses explosive seed dispersal grows in tropical forests of North and South America. The sandbox tree has earned the nickname "the dynamite tree." Its seed pod is 7 centimeters (3 inches) long and looks like the segments of a tangerine. When it's ripe, it blows apart with a loud *bang*, scattering flat seeds up to 40 meters (130 feet).

SPORES!

A family of plants known as fungi have seeds called "spores." Some fungi shoot spores into the air to be picked up by the wind and scattered about. You may have stepped on those brownish puffballs with spores that pop out in a cloud that looks like a puff of smoke. The bird's nest fungus develops a ball of spores that turns inside out and rockets its contents into the air. Rain sends the balls containing the spores flying, but the spores emerge after the balls dry out.

Mantis Shrimp

Lurking on the seafloor close to shore, a harmless-looking creature waits for prey. Crab or snail might be on the lunch menu. Both of those marine animals have a hard shell designed to stop most predators cold. It doesn't stop the mantis shrimp, however. Watch closely because it's easy to miss this creature's moves. After an explosive blow by the 15-centimeter (6-inch) long mantis shrimp, the crab or snail shell is cracked. Lunch is served!

The mantis shrimp sheds its exoskeleton to grow and to replace broken claws.

How did it happen? The mantis shrimp is named for its front claws, which it holds up in the pose of the praying mantis when it hunts. The claws have rounded, club-like ends and hinges made of "chitin" (the same material that makes up the hard covering of marine crustaceans) that can be pinched tight like a spring. A sudden release of this pent-up energy adds tremendous force to the blow. While the strike itself has explosive speed, it still might not be enough on its own to crack a tough crab shell. There seems to be more to this than meets the eye.

Zoologists studying this animal with high-speed cameras have recorded not only the explosive blow, but also the force of explosive bubbles. In an instant, when a movement so fast through the water leaves a low-pressure spot (like a cavity or hole), water becomes bubbles of vapor. As soon as normal pressure returns, the bubbles cave in so hard that they can shatter things such as crab shells. While most explosions throw force outward, the higher pressure of water in this case pushes inward to fill the cavity. The poor crab gets a double whammy—the exploding force from the mantis shrimp's club and those exploding bubbles. Just how fast is the mantis shrimp? One biologist clocked its strike at 23 meters (75 feet) per second, giving it possibly the most powerful punch of any predator on Earth.

Bombardier Beetle

It may be a small, ordinary-looking brown, black, or orange beetle. But if attacked, it packs a big surprise. The 5-centimeter (2-inch) long bombardier beetle has an unusual way to scare off would-be predators such as ants, spiders, frogs, or birds. It shoots rapid, explosive pulses of boiling hot, stinging chemicals at them. Who wouldn't run from that?

This beetle makes the nasty weapon inside its body. Its abdomen contains two chambers, one filled with the chemicals hydroquinone and hydrogen peroxide, and the other with an enzyme called peroxidase. Separately, these substances are not a problem, but mixing them causes a chemical reaction that creates oxygen, heat, and...poisonous liquid quinines that burn skin. The heat changes the liquids to gas, which builds up enough pressure to force open a nozzle at the tip of the beetle's abdomen and release a vapor cloud, often with a popping sound. In fractions of a second, the beetle can refill its chambers and shoot again. And again. In fact, the bombardier beetle can shoot 735 times per second! Watch out! This bug has amazing aim. It can shoot backward or to the side, or flip its rear guns around to blast an enemy in front of it.

How does a predator outsmart this beetle? Apparently, mice are able to grab it by the head and force the rear end into the sand so that the chemical explosion does not harm them. To go to all that trouble, mice must really enjoy a bombardier beetle snack.

If you think this clever defense method created by nature is mind-blowing, you're not alone. Scientists have taken notice. Just as humans have borrowed other ideas from nature (those burrs that stick to your clothes gave an inventor the idea for Velcro!), maybe we could borrow this powerful spray system. Scientists have studied the beetles with high-speed cameras and

The bombardier beetle can shoot its burning chemicals as far as 20 centimeters (8 inches).

even taken apart their chemical storage chambers to examine them. They learned that it takes a tiny amount of fuel and air to create the explosion. Scientists have made artificial models that work in a similar way and may now be able to use what they've learned to make safer and better delivery systems for things that need to be sprayed quickly, such as inhalers for asthma or fire extinguishers.

Cows emit large amounts of intestinal gases such as methane and ammonia.

The explosion nobody wants has several names: "fart," "flatulence," "passing gas," "breaking wind." All mammals do it. As with other explosions, gases under high pressure are suddenly released. The gas inside your lower bowel comes from food, plus nitrogen and oxygen taken in as you swallow. The large intestine adds hydrogen, carbon dioxide, and methane to the digestive process. The shortest exit for that gas is through the anus—your back door. The fart might be silent or create the sound that embarrasses you and makes you giggle— or look around for someone else to blame. Trouble is, even if there's no sound, a smell (caused by sulfur or methane in food) might give you away. *Eeeww!* Most farts are odorless, though. Good thing, since the average person might pass gas 14 to 23 times a day, even while sleeping.

EXPLODING ANIMALS

When whales die on beaches, observers can get a close-up view of these enormous marine mammals before they decompose. This whale beached in New Zealand.

Do animals ever blow up? Not normally, but some incidents have caught people's attention. Exploding whales? Exploding toads? These explosions happened on opposite sides of the world and for quite different reasons.

Sea animals die and wash up on shores around the world all the time. They usually decompose quickly as part of the natural cycle of life, with few people being aware of them. But when a whale washes ashore near a populated spot, people notice. In January 2004, a sperm whale weighing 45 tonnes (50 tons)—as much as six African elephants—died on a beach in Taiwan. While arrangements were made to move the carcass for study at a research center, bacteria began to eat away at the whale's innards, causing a huge build-up of gases. The whale was being transported on a flatbed truck when pressure from the gases inside the abdomen became too much and it suddenly exploded, splattering body bits far and wide on the street in Tainan City. Fortunately, no one was hurt by the blubber flying through the air. What caused the whale carcass to go off with such a *bang*? Decomposition is the normal rotting process that dead animals undergo, but usually scavengers will attack a carcass and this leaves holes for most gas to escape. However, this whale's skin had stayed intact, like a balloon.

Near the German city of Hamburg, other exploding critters made the news. In 2005, thousands of dead toads began turning up in a lake. Mysteriously, they seemed to have inflated to more than three times their normal size, blown up, and left pieces of their insides scattered for up to 1 meter (3 feet). With no visible reason for this strange event, biologists were left puzzled.

When a veterinarian examined the remains of the toads, he found small puncture wounds on their abdomens. The shape and location of the holes led him to likely suspects: crows. Another clue that helped crack the case was the increase in the number of crows locally. It seems that the birds had learned how to attack the toads with their sharp beaks to remove and eat the toads' livers. The toads had tried to defend themselves by puffing up to appear larger to the attacking crows. When the crows jabbed through the skin to take their liver lunch, the toads' blood vessels and lungs popped. However, unlike the sperm whale that exploded after death, the unlucky toads blew up while they were still alive.

Besides puffing itself up to look larger, the European common toad can discourage enemies by producing a toxin that gives it a bad flavor.

Decomposition begins as soon as death happens and has several stages. Once the cells die, the body's natural bacteria begin to act on tissues. They produce gases, among other things, that can swell up body cavities (such as the abdomen) until they burst. The soft tissues of the corpse continue to break down until all that remains may be bones. In time, even these will disappear. It may sound gross but it's really an efficient, natural process that recycles nutrients back into the earth so they can be reused by other life forms.

explosions
we create

DESTRUCTIVE EXPLOSIONS

Gunpowder

What a surprise it must have been! The discovery of gunpowder was likely an accident: according to one theory, someone mixed up some powders to guarantee long life but the mixture exploded instead. Gunpowder dates back to AD 900 in China and was first known as "black powder." Amazingly, it is still widely used and made in much the same way as it was originally. Gunpowder is a combination of saltpeter (potassium nitrate), sulfur, and charcoal. Saltpeter is a mineral formed by decaying animal manure. When burned, it releases large amounts of oxygen. Sulfur is mined from volcanic rock. Charcoal is the remains of burnt wood.

Wooden barrels had to be tightly made to ensure gunpowder stayed dry and did not leak.

The right amounts of these three ingredients will produce a powder called a "low explosive"—explosive enough to force a bullet from a gun barrel, but not so strong that the gun itself would be damaged. The mixture that works best is 75 percent saltpeter, 10 percent sulfur, and 15 percent charcoal. Sulfur in the mixture ignites first, creating heat to set the charcoal ablaze. Charcoal burns at a high temperature, and its heat causes the saltpeter to break apart and release oxygen. Oxygen is exactly what the sulfur and charcoal need to burn even faster and hotter. More heat, more oxygen, more burning….This rapid cycle of combustion creates a large amount of hot gases that expand.

When they first discovered gunpowder, the Chinese likely used it in simply constructed weapons. They found that a tube of bamboo loaded with gunpowder, sealed at both ends, and with a fuse to carry a flame to the gunpowder inside could cause

Sulfur, one ingredient in gunpowder, is a yellow powdery rock found naturally in volcanic areas.

damage. The first bomb? What if the front end of a container was left open and a spray of fiery powder was forced out? Flamethrowers were invented. By leaving the back end open, the gunpowder shot the whole container forward, and the rocket came into being. Eventually, an object was placed inside a tube and forced out explosively by ignited gunpowder—the technology behind guns and cannons.

By the mid-1200s, Europe knew of these adaptations for gunpowder, and it became a weapon on the battlefield. Worldwide, gunpowder has fired the guns and cannons of countless warring nations.

Gunpowder is a dangerous substance, and early gunpowder was especially unpredictable. It had to be mixed on the spot when it was needed because the ingredients separated if they were

A charge of gunpowder launched cannonballs during warfare.

combined ahead of time and moved around. If moisture got into the powders, they didn't work well. However, someone eventually discovered that a paste could be made from the three powders, mixed with a little water, and pressed into solid chunks. These were easier to transport and could be broken into smaller pieces as needed.

Gunpowder was highly dangerous to produce, so extreme precautions had to be taken in gunpowder factories. The powders were ground, mixed, and pressed under huge marble or iron wheels. To prevent friction from creating accidental sparks and setting off the powder, wooden tools were used. When horses pulled the wheels, they were not fitted with metal horseshoes, and no one was allowed to smoke in the area. Even so, massive explosions tore through the largest gunpowder plant in the United States several times during the 1800s. One eventual change to gunpowder was the addition of graphite, a mineral that helps to prevent accidental explosions ignited by static electricity.

Another change in gunpowder came in the mid-1800s, in Europe, when smokeless powder was made from a material called nitrocellulose (cellulose mixed with nitric and sulfuric acids). It changed completely to gas when lit, leaving no soot to clog the barrels of weapons and no smoke to clear from the battlefield. Smokeless powders also produce a great deal more energy than the same amount of black powder, and they are safer because they don't explode unless burned in a tightly confined space. This is the type of gunpowder produced today.

ROGER BACON

The scientific investigations of English friar and scientist Roger Bacon did not find favor with the religious leaders of the time. Around 1249, he described the devilish explosiveness of gunpowder and wrote the formula for it in a secret code. The meaning of his coded writing wasn't discovered for 650 years. However, by around 1267, gunpowder was no secret to the rest of Europe, where it became widely used on battlefields.

Dynamite

Don't drop it! That was the big fear when the oily liquid nitroglycerin was invented in 1846. It was highly dangerous to move: the slightest shock would make it explode. A nitroglycerin molecule is a complicated arrangement of loosely connected atoms. If struck suddenly, these atoms instantly rearrange themselves into carbon dioxide, nitrogen, and oxygen—gases that need hundreds of times more space than the liquid they come from. The speed at which this rearrangement produces heat and incredibly large volumes of gases creates a far more powerful explosive than gunpowder. A gunpowder explosion was fast, but a nitroglycerin blast was many times faster.

Seeing the potential in this power-packed explosive, Alfred Nobel began experimenting with ways to make it safer. He looked for a substance that would soak it up and hold it in a stable form. By mixing nitroglycerin with a soft, powdery rock called "diatomaceous earth," Nobel made an explosive that was easier to handle—with no accidental spills and unexpected explosions. Nobel called his 1867 invention "dynamite."

The first safe high-explosive material developed, dynamite could be shaped into short sticks wrapped in paper. It was the perfect shape and size for miners to use because it would fit into holes drilled into rock. They could attach a fuse long enough to let them light the fuse, then safely clear the area. Once lit, the fuse set off the small explosion of a blasting cap that triggered the much larger dynamite explosion.

While it has also been used in weapons during warfare, dynamite's main function today is in the mining, rock-quarrying, and construction industries. It's an effective way to extract minerals

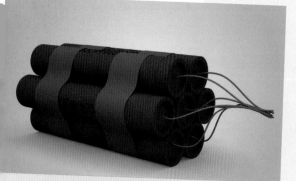

Dynamite sticks will not explode until after the fuse is lit.

and metals from the earth. If engineers need to blast a tunnel through a mountain for a new highway or railroad—or to deepen a harbor—dynamite gives the explosive solution. From such major construction projects as these to blasting rock for gravel, Nobel's invention of a safer high explosive has proven its worth.

SUGAR CAN EXPLODE!

Sugar is nothing like nitroglycerin, but surprise—sugar *can* explode. You already know it burns easily: hold a marshmallow over a campfire and it will blacken quickly as it flames up. If enough powdered sugar, flour, fine sawdust, grain dust—or almost any fine dust, like coal dust—is floating free in the air in an enclosed space, a single spark can set off an explosion. Only one grain may catch fire but that's enough to light others nearby. The flames will leap explosively from grain to grain through the dust hanging in the air. If that dust cloud is inside a building such as a flour mill...*boom!*

When it comes to winter fun—and safety—dynamite can play a part, too. Imagine an avalanche suddenly roars down a mountainside, wiping out trees and burying everything in its path under tons of snow. These slides happen when a thick snow layer builds up on the slope. Crystals of snow can no longer stick together because of the excess weight and so they let go. The shock wave of a loud sound is enough to set off a slide. However, snow-safety experts can use this knowledge and dynamite to their advantage, as a method of avalanche control when snow builds up above a highway or railroad, or near runs at a ski resort. Triggering small avalanches on purpose when everyone is safely out of the way can help prevent larger slides that could be deadly.

Bombs

Bombs are one of humanity's deadliest inventions. Not long after the invention of gunpowder in AD 900, bombs likely began as simple metal containers filled with gunpowder, lit with a wick, and thrown at an enemy. Although these early bombs were unpredictable—often exploding before they were thrown or before reaching their target—the idea of a portable explosive device that would be sudden and devastating didn't go away. By World War I, the technology had evolved so that small bombs could be tossed from the relative safety of a trench. Many types of bombs have been created since.

Bombs now can be designed to explode on impact or they can be set off by a time-delayed ignition system. In the first case, the bomb explodes when it hits a target. The force of the impact sets off a detonator that ignites the explosive material inside. These bombs can be thrown, dropped from aircraft, attached to the tip of a missile, or rocket-fired from a launcher.

In contrast, a time-delayed bomb has an inner fuse that allows the person using the bomb enough time to find safety. Hand-grenades use a firing pin that, when pulled, releases a spring-loaded trigger onto a detonator; the trigger touches the detonator and creates a spark that ignites explosive material inside the small bomb. Several seconds pass between these actions to give the person time to throw the grenade. With depth charges, water pressure is the trigger for the detonation. These bombs were dropped from battleships during World War II if an enemy submarine was known to be lurking below. When the bomb container was thrown overboard, it would sink, and at a certain depth, the increased water pressure would trigger the explosion. By the time of the blast, the ship that launched the depth charge could be safely out of the way. Land mines, still in use today in

A soldier in World War II practices throwing a small time-delayed bomb—the hand-grenade.

some parts of the world, are sometimes triggered by pressure changes—if stepped on or driven over. However, some land mines are designed with trip wires that are left sticking out on top when they are buried in fields or along roads. Trip-wired land mines will go off when something catches the wire and pulls it, like the firing pin on a grenade. A recent development, some bombs can be set off from a distance by radios or cell phones, operating much like the remote signal that turns your television on and off. The signal triggers a detonator in the bomb, and that small explosion ignites additional explosive material for the big blast.

Bombs vary in how they are made and their results. Some cause terrible injury or loss of life by breaking apart and scattering sharp pieces of metal, called "shrapnel." Others explode with fire or smoke, noise, or poisonous gas. If the bomb contains nuclear material, the explosion is much more disastrous.

One example stands out in history as the most devastating explosions from bombs. On August 6 and August 9, 1945, nuclear

A B-17 Flying Fortress drops its bombs over an enemy target during World War II.

An enormous mushroom-shaped cloud rises over Nagasaki, Japan. Two nuclear bombs forced the country to surrender in World War II.

Since gunpowder and dynamite were invented, explosives have been developed in many forms. Complex chemical mixtures are sometimes known by easier-to-remember initials such as TNT, RDX, and HMX. Along with picric acid and other explosives, TNT was on board the *Mont-Blanc* when it blew up in Halifax harbor. Gelignite—a mixture that includes nitroglycerin and nitrocellulose, and that was invented by Alfred Nobel in 1875—was the first "plastic explosive" and is used today in construction by engineers and in modern-day warfare. Gelignite, Semtex, and C-4 are called plastic explosives because they can be safely molded by hand into different shapes. Plastic explosives are used for demolition and by terrorist groups.

bombs were dropped on the Japanese cities of Hiroshima and Nagasaki when Japan refused to surrender during World War II. The massive explosions released blinding light and a searing blast of heat that killed many people instantly and destroyed buildings. (In Hiroshima, nearly every building within 1.6 kilometers [1 mile] of the city's ground zero was destroyed.) Many more people died as a huge firestorm erupted, and even more died that year from burns, radiation, or disease. From the bombings to the end of 1945, about 140,000 people died in Hiroshima and 80,000 in Nagasaki—about half on the bombing days. In years following the war, injuries or long-term effects of radiation continued to kill people. Even 45 years later, in 1990, some cancer deaths were blamed on the bombings. In a recent ceremony of remembrance in Hiroshima, it was noted that almost 260,000 people had died in that city alone since the bombing.

THE HALIFAX EXPLOSION

Buildings were blown apart by the massive explosion in Halifax harbor.

On the morning of December 6, 1917, children in Halifax, Nova Scotia, were getting ready for school. When two ships collided in the harbor at 8:45 a.m., many children and adults ran to the waterfront. A crowd grew to watch the fire on the deck of one ship near Pier 6. No one expected that, at 9:05 a.m., a massive explosion would rock the city—an explosion that was the largest ever artificial explosion before the nuclear bombs were dropped on Japan during World War II.

In 1917, the port city of Halifax was where ships gathered before sailing east across the Atlantic to Europe. The ships carried troops, food, munitions, and other supplies to the European countries engaged in World War I. German submarines prowled the waters off the coast, but the city's large harbor was protected by a double gateway of anti-submarine netting. The gate was closed at night and only opened in daylight to allow ships in and out. Because it was wartime, even ships carrying explosives were allowed access only during the day. Once inside the gates, ships would enter the outer harbor and pass through a narrow channel (the Narrows) to get to the inner harbor (the Bedford Basin).

The cargo ship *Imo* was loaded with emergency relief supplies destined for Belgium. The *Imo* had stayed in the Basin overnight on December 5 because its supply of fuel had arrived too late for it to sail before the gates closed.

The *Mont-Blanc* had sailed from New York to Halifax, where it was to join a group of ships sailing east. Its destination was Bordeaux, France, and it carried about

2,900 tonnes (3,196 tons) of explosives and flammable material, some stored in drums on the deck. The *Mont-Blanc* had arrived on December 5 after dusk, too late to enter the harbor, so it anchored outside the gates.

Ships have to obey rules of the road just like cars do. However, in the congested harbor, the scene was set for a series of tragic mistakes that morning. As the *Imo* left the crowded Basin through the Narrows, it was forced off course. At the same time, the *Mont-Blanc* entered the narrow channel properly, only to find the *Imo* on a collision course. Unable to avoid each other, the ships collided. Sparks flew. Fire erupted, fueled by the material on the *Mont-Blanc*'s deck. The *Mont-Blanc*'s crew thought their ship would explode quickly and immediately left in the lifeboats, leaving the *Mont-Blanc* adrift. It reached Pier 6, spreading the fire. Despite frantic efforts to put out the fire and to tow the ship back to mid-harbor, within a mere 20 minutes, the *Mont-Blanc*'s cargo of munitions erupted in an explosive fireball.

The shock wave, felt hundreds of kilometers away, flattened much of the northern side of the city and swept small boats across the harbor on a tidal wave. People were hit by flying shrapnel, buried under rubble as buildings collapsed, or burned in fires that broke out when wood stoves overturned. Crews aboard other ships, as well as the crowd that arrived to watch the fire near Pier 6, were

The explosion tore away this ship's superstructure and beached it in the harbor.

killed instantly. Many watching through windows suffered eye injuries from flying glass. A fierce snowstorm the next day followed by a sudden drop in temperatures made rescue efforts difficult, but Halifax personnel were helped by the American Red Cross, which sent doctors, nurses, and supplies on two trains from Boston. Despite all these efforts, 2,000 people died in the tragedy, including 88 children from the nearby Richmond School.

Halifax still welcomes ships from around the world into its deep-water harbor. Many city memorials recall that tragic day in 1917. Each Christmas, the Nova Scotia government sends a large fir tree to Boston as a "thank you" for the help offered after the city of Halifax was devastated by the huge explosion.

CONSTRUCTIVE EXPLOSIONS

5

Ripple Rock

Explorer Captain George Vancouver warned about a pair of sharp, underwater rock peaks in 1792, when he mapped Discovery Passage, between mainland British Columbia and Vancouver Island. Ripple Rock lay directly in the path of ships sailing a waterway 5 kilometers (3 miles) long and known as Seymour Narrows. Only about 750 meters (2,460 feet) wide at its narrowest point, the channel had dangerous tidal currents that created whirlpools and unusually turbulent water around the rocks. What's worse, at low tide, the two rocks were covered by only 3 meters (9 feet) of water—about as high as a basketball hoop.

In 1875, the captain of a side-wheel steamer heading for Alaska made a bad choice: he attempted to take the ship, the USS *Saranac,* through the Seymour Narrows at low tide. The *Saranac* was tossed about like a toy in the currents swirling around the top of the underwater mountain, and it became the first large ship lost to Ripple Rock. Although everyone on board the *Saranac* survived the sinking, at least 110 other people met their deaths at this spot. Over the years, the rough waters proved too much for about 120 vessels, and "Old Rip" earned a reputation with sailors. Something had to be done about Ripple Rock.

The Canadian government first gave the go-ahead to remove the treacherous peaks in 1942. Between 1943 and 1958, several attempts were made, using floating barges and holes drilled for explosive charges, but they lost against the current's unrelenting power. Ripple Rock was not about to give up easily.

Blowing up Ripple Rock cleared a shipping hazard from the passage that explorer Captain George Vancouver had called "one of the vilest stretches of water in the world."

A new idea was proposed: if it couldn't be removed from above, what about from below? This idea led to a major operation that took over two years and involved digging down, across, and up into the mountain peaks. Seventy-five hard-rock miners dug a 175-meter (575-foot) vertical shaft down into nearby Maud Island and a 162-meter (530-foot) tunnel out under Seymour Narrows. The next step was to drill twin tunnels, each 91 meters (328 feet), upward into the rock peaks. While the drilling was going on, explosion experts tested various kinds of detonating material to see what would work the best. A product called Primacord, a thin cord made of textile and with a center of highly powerful explosives, was the answer. This kind of detonation cord—or "det cord"—is still used today.

Inside Ripple Rock, 1,270 tonnes (1,400 tons) of explosives were planted in hundreds of holes. Engineering geologists were taking no chances on failure this time. All that blasting material created one of the largest planned non-nuclear explosions ever.

For the blast scheduled on April 5, 1958, everyone was evacuated within a radius of about 5 kilometers (3 miles). Authorities feared that the massive explosion would trigger an earthquake or a tsunami (tidal wave). In fact, people in the surrounding area said that they felt barely a tremor and the sound of the blast was muffled by the water. However, a remote camera set up 1 kilometer (.62 miles) away recorded the 9:31 a.m. blast: within 10 seconds, the explosion sent rock bits flying 300 meters (984 feet) into the air and caused only a small tidal wave that fizzled out quickly.

Was Ripple Rock gone? Sort of. The mountaintop was flattened so that 14 meters (46 feet) of water—more than enough to cover a stack of four school buses—conceals it at low tide. It's safe to sail over; in fact, cruise ships sailing the Inside Passage, bound for Alaska, sail over it all the time. Now, however, it's safest to tackle this legendary stretch of water between tide changes, when there is little or no current. Even so, people who sail the route when the tides shift talk of the unruly current and nerve-wracking passage through this National Historic Site. Maybe the ghosts of Ripple Rock still lurk below the surface.

PANAMA CANAL

More than 30 million kilograms (67 million pounds) of dynamite, 84,000 people, and 34 years—that's what it took to build the Panama Canal. To open this 81-kilometer (50-mile) long passage in 1914, workers blasted through barriers of rock, like the Continental Divide, built dams, and created artificial lakes and a series of locks that raise ships almost 26 meters (85 feet) as they sail between the Pacific and Atlantic oceans.

Explosive Demolition

While an "explosion" usually throws material outward (not so good if you don't want to wreck anything nearby), an "implosion" will cause a structure to collapse inward before it falls down.

Explosive demolition—implosion—is used to safely bring down an old structure within the space where it was built, leaving nothing else around it touched. Walls will fall with the help of gravity when supports that hold them up are strategically removed with explosives. To the bystander, it might look as if someone directly above the building punched it down.

Let's say you want to get rid of a 20-story downtown building, one closely surrounded by other tall buildings. You'd start by calling a skilled demolition company. The demolition experts would study the plans for the building to see how it had been constructed. If the support structures—pillars and beams—are concrete, they will need to be drilled and packed with dynamite. If they are steel, a faster explosive (such as one called RDX) will be needed to slice through them, along with dynamite to push them over.

Next, experts would decide where to set their explosive charges. Before blasting day, they might test their plan on models to see how well it will work. Think of a building as a house of cards: take out just the right cards in the right order and the rest will collapse neatly. For example, detonate the central supports in a building, and the outer walls should fall into the center, or collapse a collection of towers in the right order and they will fall inward against each other. Usually, explosive charges are set on the first one or two floors, and they may also be set on several other levels of the building to help break up material into smaller pieces as it drops.

The amount of explosives needed is calculated carefully. Too much, and debris might fly outside the building being imploded.

TALLEST BUILDING IMPLODED

The tallest building to be imploded was Detroit's 26-story Hudson's Department Store—demolished in 1998. With a length of 817 meters (2,680 feet), a bridge on Interstate 80 at Boston Mills, Ohio, was the longest structure dropped by controlled demolition.

Building a new railway line and adjacent parking lot in Johannesburg, South Africa, meant first imploding buildings to make room.

Supports inside and at the ground level are blown apart first.

Inner walls collapse and the buildings begin to sink.

The outer walls fall toward the center.

Dust hides the final moments of the implosion.

The buildings have been safely reduced to a pile of rubble that will be trucked away.

Not enough, and the structure may not collapse completely. No one wants to venture inside a half-demolished building to check what went wrong! All the experts want to see when the job is done is a neat pile of rubble that can be trucked away.

When the charges are in place, blasting caps are connected to fuses ready to set off with an electrical current. Detonation may be timed with longer or slower burning fuses to make parts of the building blow earlier or later. Last, but not least, a video camera may be set up to record the implosion. This makes a good record for the company to study for future demolition jobs.

Ready? Stand back…stand *way* back! Once the fuse is ignited, it takes only seconds for the construction work of many months (or years) to disappear with a *bang* in a cloud of dust.

PREPARING TO IMPLODE

Preparation for an implosion must be thorough. One way to prepare is to clean up—really! Everything that can be easily removed from inside the building—including materials that may be recycled (for example, glass or copper wire)—must be taken away before any explosives are used. Walls that only separate rooms but don't hold up the weight of a ceiling can be taken out, while any support pillars can be weakened with sledgehammers. Another way to prepare is to check the weather. It's best to do implosions on a clear day so the shock wave from such a huge blast is more likely to travel straight up. If it's cloudy, moisture in the atmosphere can force it sideways, perhaps breaking nearby windows.

Internal Combustion Engine

Starting the family car won't blow it up, but it does create an explosion. It's not one that you can see or that will destroy anything. Instead, it's the kind of explosion that you can put to work. Deep inside the engine, fuel ignited inside an enclosed space explodes, releasing energy. This energy is harnessed to move the car. How does it work? It's a process called "combustion" and inside the car engine, it's called "internal combustion."

In an internal combustion engine, gasoline and air are rapidly burned in a confined space called a "combustion chamber." The combustion chamber is a cylinder that is closed at one end and has a sliding piece called a "piston." Exploding fuel inside the cylinder creates gases that heat up, expanding quickly to create extreme pressure, which then moves the piston. One hundred explosions per minute keep the piston quickly sliding, or stroking, in and out. The other end of the piston is connected by a rod to a crankshaft that rotates when the piston pushes it. The crankshaft turns the driveshaft, which turns the axles, which hold the wheels… to move the car.

The fuel supply for the engine is kept in a separate tank. It is pumped, as needed, into a device called a "carburetor," which mixes the gasoline with the right amount of oxygen to make it burn well. The resulting vapor enters the combustion cylinder. To ignite this fuel, a spark plug uses a high-voltage current from a battery to create a spark. In modern cars, the carburetor has been replaced by an electronic fuel-injection system that gives better control over the amount of gas used. This means less wasted gas, or exhaust, is left to expel from the cylinder. Many small engines, such as lawn mowers and chainsaws, still use a carburetor.

This cutaway shows an engine's combustion chamber, where fuel is ignited and explodes.

THE FOUR-STROKE ENGINE

Step on the gas pedal of a car, and you're speeding up the rate of the explosions! All that exploding makes the engine hot, so the cylinder must be cooled from the outside by air or water. Sometimes part of the gas and air mixture makes it out of the cylinder unburned and into the car's exhaust system. Hear that loud *pop*? That's an explosion, too. It's called a "backfire."

THE 'OTTO' CYCLE GAS ENGINE

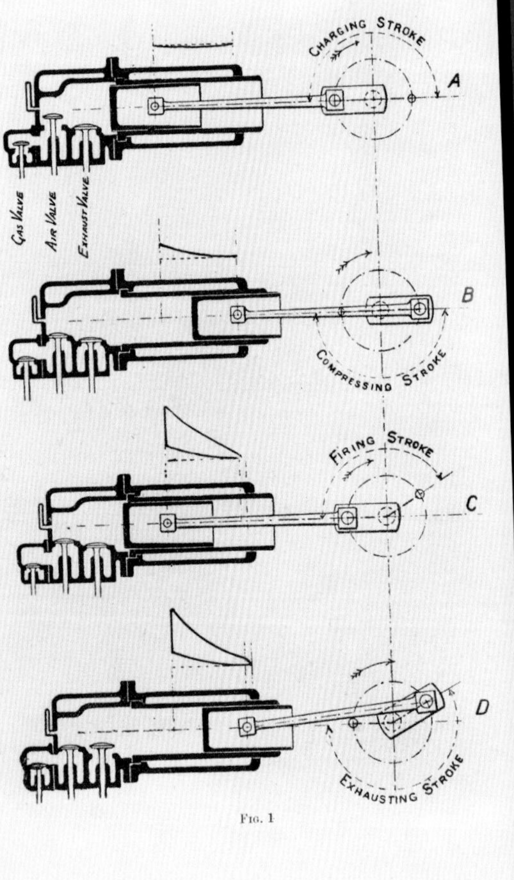

CHARGING STROKE — A

GAS VALVE AIR VALVE EXHAUST VALVE

COMPRESSING STROKE — B

FIRING STROKE — C

EXHAUSTING STROKE — D

FIG. 1

In the late 1600s, scientists first tried using fuel in enclosed spaces to produce energy to run an engine. Gunpowder proved too dangerous, so for the next 200 years, inventors in various European countries experimented with different fuels: hydrogen, steam, and coal gas. None proved practical; for example, steam engines added too much weight to a road vehicle, but worked well in train engines. Finally, in 1876, Nicolaus Otto built the first successful four-stroke internal combustion gasoline engine: it took four slides of the piston to bring in the fuel, create pressure, ignite it, and expel it. Soon after, Gottlieb Daimler came up with an early version of a gasoline engine. He built the world's first four-wheel motor vehicle in 1885. Another inventor, Karl Benz, got the first patent for a gas-fueled car. The two inventors teamed up in 1926 to form a company, Daimler-Benz, best known for its Mercedes-Benz vehicles. Today, either gasoline or diesel is used in internal combustion engines. But the search is still on for inexpensive and non-polluting fuels that can be made from renewable sources, such as corn oil.

AIR BAGS

An explosion could save your life. Your family car is equipped with cushiony air bags designed to stop you from being injured in a collision at speeds of 16–24 kilometers (10–15 miles) per hour. A sensor causes an electrical connection to close, triggering a mixture of chemicals that creates a large amount of hot nitrogen gas. That causes an air bag to burst from its container in the steering wheel, dashboard, or door, filling the space between passengers and the hard interior of the car. When its job is done, the bag quickly deflates as the gas leaks through tiny holes in the nylon fabric.

MOUNT RUSHMORE

Dynamite sticks as short as 2.5 centimeters (1 inch) were used to carefully remove unwanted rock from the carving surface of Mount Rushmore.

Dynamite is an explosive tool for removing rocks that stand in the way of construction projects, such as roads and tunnels. But can it be used to create works of art? A sculptor named Gutzon Borglum thought so. In 1927, he began to carve the faces of four American presidents—George Washington, Thomas Jefferson, Theodore Roosevelt, and Abraham Lincoln—18 meters (60 feet) tall, side by side onto Mount Rushmore, a wall of granite in South Dakota.

Working on such a huge scale with hard material took more than just the talents of a sculptor. Before Borglum could begin his work with a chisel, huge chunks of the rock had to be blasted away. Borglum hired over 360 miners from the nearby Black Hills who knew how to drill and blast rock. A staircase of 506 steps and 45 ramps was built to allow the men and supplies to reach the top of the mountain.

Creating the general shape of the heads was the first problem. The miners hung over the rock face in harnesses, lowered from the top by hand-winched cables. When they wanted to move up, down, or sideways to reach their work spaces, the harnessed men signaled the cable operators above them. Guided by markings taken from scale models, the miners placed sticks of dynamite in holes drilled in the top layer of granite. It took great skill to use the explosives in a way that would remove *only* the intended rock and do so as quickly as possible. Dynamite took out almost 90 percent of

CRAZY HORSE

© Crazy Horse Memorial

Just 27 kilometers (17 miles) away from Mount Rushmore, a statue of Lakota Chief Crazy Horse and his horse will stand 172 meters (563 feet) high on a rocky crag. The Crazy Horse Memorial was begun in 1948 with a mission "to honor the culture, tradition, and living heritage of North American Indians." The face of Crazy Horse was dedicated in 1998, but the work on his horse has no completion date. You can visit the site and watch as the rock is blasted away.

Workers hang in harnesses as they shape the face of the first American president, George Washington.

FUN FACT

George Washington's eyes are 3.3 meters (11 feet) wide, with pupils 56 centimeters (22 inches) wide, and his nose is 6 meters (20 feet) long. Thomas Jefferson's mouth is 5.4 meters (18 feet) wide or about three times as long as your bed.

the 408 tonnes (450 tons) of rock removed. It was set off at lunchtime and late afternoon so no workers would be harmed. Amazingly, not one life was lost during this tricky construction project.

The next task was drilling a layer of rock with jackhammers to create a honeycomb of many holes 2.5–5 centimeters (1–2 inches) deep. Imagine bouncing around on a rock face as the force of the jackhammer pushes at you! The workers held themselves steady with chains linked to the rock face. Next, the rock between the holes was chipped away until only about 15 centimeters (6 inches) remained before reaching the final finished surface.

Last, out came the smaller tools: pneumatic hammers and chisels. The miners and drillers had no experience with sculpting rock so Borglum, the artist, did the fine detail work, with some help from his son. The sculpture of George Washington was dedicated on July 4, 1934. It took until 1941 (with many weather delays) and almost a million dollars to complete this enormous memorial in stone.

PRIMACORD

Stone carving with explosives has changed since Mount Rushmore was blasted. Engineers now use Primacord and other "det cord"—a detonating material that explodes over a much wider area than the same amount of dynamite would. Rock is removed more effectively by packing the cord into a series of drill holes set close together. An electronic system sets off the charge and is precisely timed for the best effect.

Fireworks

Bang! Ooooh! Aaaah!
If you've watched a fireworks display, you've been amazed by the brilliance and the spectacular combinations of reds, blues, greens, and yellows. You've seen the night sky fill with motion, as patterns and designs made of light form and dissolve, perhaps in time to music. The powerful *bangs* and *booms* probably made your ears ring.

Today's pyrotechnicians are artists who create shooting stars or sparks, dazzling particles of confetti trickling from the sky, or rainbow fountains of liquid light. Fireworks may spiral in pinwheels or burst toward you like a giant flower opening its petals. It can take many hours to set up a large fireworks display that only lasts minutes.

Fireworks have come a long way from the first discovery, most likely in China around 200 BC, that tossing a piece of green bamboo into a fire would make it blow up. The air and sap in the plant would naturally heat and expand with a *bang*. After gunpowder was accidentally invented by mixing saltpeter, sulfur, and charcoal (around AD 900), the bamboo could be purposely loaded with explosive material. The loud *crack* was sure to scare off anything evil lurking in the night. No wonder the idea was used in warfare as the Chinese fought off Mongol invasions. Bamboo tubes were attached to arrows, lit, and launched at the enemy as early rockets. It didn't take long to find other uses for these startling objects. A Chinese monk living in Hunan province and named Li Tian is believed to have invented the first fireworks, since used in Chinese New Year celebrations and other festivities.

Pyrotechnicians find creative ways to show off the latest firework styles and colors.

The major fireworks companies in the United States are still run by the Italian families who started them. In 1870, the Gruccis set up a company in New York, and in 1893, the Zambellis opened a plant in Pennsylvania. Each family closely guards its secret formulas, passing them along from older to younger generations.

What better way to ensure happiness and good fortune for new beginnings than by frightening off those evil spirits!

Knowledge of gunpowder and fireworks may have been brought from Asia to Europe by Marco Polo, in the 13th century. With the earliest fireworks, noise was the desired effect. But artisans soon saw exciting ways to play with light. In Italy, chemists discovered that using time-delayed fuses allowed them to send shells high in the air before they exploded in fountains of sparks. Colors were created by adding metals or salts, such as copper for blue, calcium for orange, and a chlorine-barium mix for green.

Most fireworks have a basic design that consists of the shell, explosive material in a container, and a fuse. Usually, three separate portions of explosives (charges) are needed: one to lift the shell high into the air, another that will cause it to burst open and scatter sparks, and a third to create the loud *bang*. Several containers, each with its own fuse, can be combined within one shell, with the explosions timed to release different colors and shapes. Modern firework makers experiment with chemicals for

Slow-burning sparklers are made from chemicals molded onto a stick. When they are lit, metal powder creates the bright sparks.

new vibrant colors, fireworks that burn hotter and faster, and even sharper blasts that echo in the night.

When pyrotechnicians use electronic fuses and a computer, they can signal detonation from a firing panel on the ground. Each firework shell has a metal tip. An electrical current is sent along a wire to the tip, igniting a spark. The spark sets off a fuse and the shell is shot into the air. The firings can be coordinated so each shell explodes at a precise moment. Now you know how fireworks can be made to dance to music!

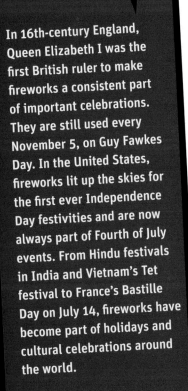

FESTIVALS

In 16th-century England, Queen Elizabeth I was the first British ruler to make fireworks a consistent part of important celebrations. They are still used every November 5, on Guy Fawkes Day. In the United States, fireworks lit up the skies for the first ever Independence Day festivities and are now always part of Fourth of July events. From Hindu festivals in India and Vietnam's Tet festival to France's Bastille Day on July 14, fireworks have become part of holidays and cultural celebrations around the world.

Special Effects

You're wide-eyed, watching the latest high-action movie where the alien spaceships are closing in to blast at Earthling targets and blow them sky high. Or maybe the hero is pinned down by a hail of bullets thudding into walls or ricocheting off cars. Dazzling flashes, brilliant fireballs, ground-shaking *bangs*, and clouds of smoke all have you breathlessly gripping the seat. You know this isn't real; it's just a movie. But it sure looks real. How do they do it?

In the world of special effects, or SFX, it's often hard to tell which explosions are the faked ones. The car that you saw blow up in a fiery collision really *did* blow up, but did the car's impact cause the explosion? More likely it was a trick of the pyrotechnical experts. A small bomb filled with black powder might be set off by an electronic fuse to blast the structurally weakened vehicle apart, while a gasoline fireball would be waiting to burst at precisely the right moment. Combine that explosion with an actor thrown into the air and you're likely imagining a narrow escape, right? Wrong. A stunt person may be tossed high with the help of an explosive charge under one end of a springboard hidden nearby.

Of course, moviemakers can't fire real bullets at people, even though bullets were once used to fire at objects in the scenery. For low-tech SFX, small capsules made of gelatin and filled with fake "blood" will burst on impact when fired from an air gun. If the capsules are to be shot at a wall, they can release dust to resemble a puff of plaster powder, or they might shed silver paint to look like metal splinters on a car. As a SFX trick, the squib is more high tech. A "squib" is a small explosive device that looks like a fuse with a wire hanging out. If it is planted in a well-camouflaged hole in the wall or the ground before the scene is filmed and the wire is connected to an electrical source, the squib explodes with noise, smoke, or sparks. Sometimes hundreds of

Did this explosion really launch the actor into the air, or was it all part of the trickery of SFX?

squibs are used in a single scene to create the effects of machine-gun fire. With the addition of a metal plate behind it for safety, a squib attached to an actor can rip open a bag of "blood" and bits of meat for the realistic look of a ghastly bullet wound.

With skill and imagination, expert filmmakers have become better and better at fooling us into believing that what we see and hear is real. There are several ways to create a convincing large explosion for a film scene. A real explosion filmed on location using black powder or gasoline bombs might be dangerous or costly. However, small-scale models of objects— including replicas of well-known buildings—can be blown up, and tricks with film speed and sizes of camera lenses can make this look real. If live action can't be used—after all, there are no actual spaceship battles going on between aliens and Earthlings— computer images can do the job. Computer-generated imagery, or digital animation, lets moviemakers create, with the click of a mouse, heart-stopping illusions of explosions to thrill the audience.

In fact, the computer is now a favorite tool for special effects. Using software to produce digital images, digital artists can create all the explosive action in a film. Beginning with video of an actual explosion, an artist might change the footage by adding or subtracting dust clouds or by exaggerating flames or fireballs. Those images might be added by computer to a scene shot earlier with actors working in a safe, fire-free area. Once the layers are matched, it is impossible to tell that it didn't all happen at the same time.

Next time you see a building ripped apart or a spectacular and fiery collision at the movies, wonder at the imagination and skill of the technician or digital artist, and enjoy the SFX.

Selected Bibliography

Britt, Robert Roy. "What Is a Solar Maximum and What Happens?" space.com online, January 31, 2000, <http://www.space.com/scienceastronomy/solarsystem/solar_max_sidebar_000131.html>.

Cowen, Ron. "Farthest Bang: A Burst That Goes the Distance." *Science News* 168:12 (September 17, 2005), page 179.

Flemming, David B. *Explosion in Halifax Harbour*. Halifax: Formac, 2004.

Flynn, Mike. *The Great Airships: The Tragedies and Triumphs, from the* Hindenburg *to the Cargo Carriers of the New Millennium*. London: Carlton, 1999.

Fussell, Betty Harper. *The Story of Corn*. New York: Alfred A. Knopf, 1992.

Gribbin, John R., and Mary Gribbin. *Stardust*. London: Penguin, 2000.

Hamilton, Jake. *Special Effects in Film and Television*. New York: DK Publishing, 1998.

Harris, Tom. "How Building Implosions Work." HowStuffWorks.com online, < http://www.howstuffworks.com/building-implosion.htm >.

Kelly, Jack. *Gunpowder: Alchemy, Bombards and Pyrotechnics. The History of the Explosive That Changed the World*. New York: Basic Books, 2004.

Leete, Jeremy. "The Taming of the Rock." *Vancouver Island Abound Outdoor Pages* online, < http://www.vancouverislandabound.com/tamingof.htm >.

Lipman, Marvin M. "Intestinal Gas: A Right of Passage." Consumer Reports Health.org online, June 2007, < http://www.consumerreports.org/health/medical-conditions-treatments/intestinal-gas/overview/0607_intestinal_gas_ov.htm >.

Meincke, Mark. *Complete Guide to Stationary Gas Engines*. Osceola, WI: Motorbooks International, 1996.

Mosher, Dave. "Crater Could Solve 1908 Tunguska Meteor Mystery." space.com online, June 26, 2007, <http://www.space.com/scienceastronomy/070626_st_tunguska_crater.html >.

Ochmanski, Lorianne. "Bombardier Beetle Blasts Spray Technology into the Future." *Plexus Encyclopedia of Medicine, Science, and Technology* 5:69 (April 28, 2008).

Patek, S.N., W.L. Korff, and R.L. Caldwell. "Biomechanics: Deadly Strike Mechanism of Mantis Shrimp." *Nature* 428 (April 22, 2004), pages 819–20.

Seife, Charles. *Alpha and Omega: The Search for the Beginning and End of the Universe*. New York: Viking, 2003.

Simons, Paul. "An Explosive Start for Plants: Plants Get Up to Some Ingenious Tricks and Aerial Acrobatics to Ensure Their Survival." *New Scientist* 1854 (January 2, 1993).

Smith, Rex Alan. *The Carving of Mount Rushmore*. New York: Abbeville, 1994.

Sohn, Emily. "Popping to Perfection." *Science News for Kids* online, May 4, 2005, < http://www.sciencenewsforkids.org/articles/20050504/Feature1.asp >.

Van Dyk, Schuyler D. "What Are Supernovae?" <http://spider.ipac.caltech.edu/staff/vandyk/supernova.html >.

White, Meagan. "Explosions in Space." Firstscience.com online, June 8, 2006, < http://www.kalin-bg.com/meagan/08062006.html >.

Further Reading

Berry, Dana. *Smithsonian Intimate Guide to the Cosmos: Visualizing the New Realities of Space*. Vancouver: Greystone/Madison, 2005.

Branley, Franklin M. *Superstar: The Supernova of 1987*. New York: Crowell, 1990.

Cho, Shinta. *The Gas We Pass: The Story of Farts*. New York: Kane/Miller, 1994.

De Paola, Tomie. *The Popcorn Book*. New York: Holiday House, 1978.

Dotz, Warren. *Firecrackers: The Art and History*. Berkeley, CA: Ten Speed Press, 2000.

Downer, John. *Weird Nature: An Astonishing Exploration of Nature's Strangest Behavior*. Willowdale, ON: Firefly Books, 2002.

Gallant, Roy A. *Geysers: When Earth Roars*. New York: Franklin Watts, 1997.

Hamilton, Jake. *Special Effects in Film and Television*. New York: DK Publishing, 1998.

Information Resource Center. "History." MountStHelens.com online, < http://www.mountsthelens.com/history-1.html >.

Kitz, Janet. *December 1917: Re-Visiting the Halifax Explosion*. Halifax: Nimbus, 2006.

Liss, Helene. *Demolition: The Art of Demolishing, Dismantling, Imploding, Toppling and Razing*. New York: Blackdog and Leventhal, 2000.

Moncure, Jane Belk. *How Seeds Travel: Popguns and Parachutes*. Chicago: Child's World, 1990.

Oleksy, Walter G. *Mapping the Skies*. New York: Franklin Watts, 2002.

Reynolds, Michael D. *Falling Stars: A Guide to Meteors and Meteorites*. Mechanicsburg, PA: Stackpole, 2001.

Santella, Andrew. *Mount Rushmore*. New York: Children's Press, 1999.

Tanaka, Shelley. *The Disaster of the* Hindenburg*: The Last Flight of the Greatest Airship Ever Built*. New York: Scholastic/Madison, 1993.

"Universe 101: Big Bang Theory." NASA (US National Aeronautics and Space Administration) online, < http://map.gsfc.nasa.gov/universe/bb_theory.html >.

Index

Photo Credits

Acknowledgments

My thanks to Carolyn L. Driedger, Hydrologist/Outreach Coordinator with the Cascades Volcano Observatory in Vancouver, Washington, for sharing her knowledge of volcanic mudflows.

Berlin reptile specialist Dr. Frank Mutschmann's response to an elusive detail on toads was most appreciated.

Thanks also to the staff of the Sorrento Branch, Okanagan Regional Library, where much of my research begins, for their persistent efforts to secure resources for me by interlibrary loan.

About the Author

Gillian Richardson grew up in Ontario and has lived on Canada's Atlantic and Pacific coasts and on the prairies. She now lives near Shuswap Lake in British Columbia. A writer and teacher, she combines her passions for reading, nature study, and investigating how things work. She has visited four volcanoes, witnessed geysers erupt, and seen seed pods explode. Popcorn is one of her favorite snacks.